CONTENTS

What **I**s **I**t?

Every day someone somewhere is taking one of the following substances. What might each of these be? The answers are given at the bottom of the page.

A *The English love it! A brown liquid. A few take it on its own but most prefer to take it with something added.*

B *In the past someone was heard to say 'You've found this new stuff made of old leaves? What do you say you do with it? You roll it up, put it between paper, stick it in your mouth . . . and then you burn it? You can't be serious!'.*

C *A white powder, once thought to be a favourite with the jet set. Usually snorted.*

D *Some people compete to see how much they can take. They have been known to devote a whole evening to visiting as many places as possible, where this is available.*

E *If you can get them, they're easy enough to take, but one in five users then become dependent on them.*

All of these are drugs. Most references to drugs that you see in newspapers, magazines and on TV, focus on illegal drugs, but the most commonly used drugs are in fact legal and socially acceptable.

If we think of 'drugs' in the widest sense, including alcohol, cigarettes and drugs which are bought over the counter, then we all have some experience of drug taking. It may be first-hand experience, in that we may ourselves have taken a particular drug, or it may be second-hand, in that we have picked up ideas and knowledge about certain drugs from elsewhere, for example from people you know or from the media.

▓ ACTIVITIES ▓▓▓▓▓▓▓▓▓▓▓▓▓▓▓▓▓▓▓▓▓▓▓▓▓▓▓▓▓▓▓

These activities may help you work out how much you already know and how you feel about drug taking.

» Work in pairs, if possible and try to think of a word connected with drugs for each letter of the alphabet. A few examples are given at the top of the next page.

Answers: A = tea B = tobacco C = cocaine D = beer E = sleeping pills

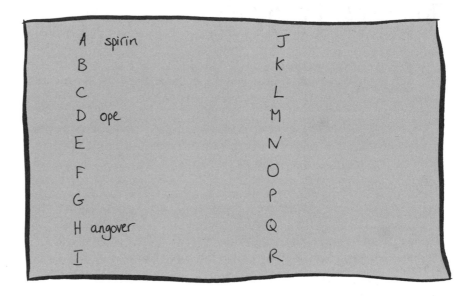

A	spirin	J	
B		K	
C		L	
D	ope	M	
E		N	
F		O	
G		P	
H	angover	Q	
I		R	

≫ Join with another pair and compare your results, seeing if you can group the words in any way. The following questions might help:

How many words were the names of drugs?

How many were street or slang terms?

How many described how a drug is taken?

How many were connected with the effects of drug taking?

How many showed drugs as negative or harmful?

How many showed drugs in a good light?

As a result of doing this, you might want to check your knowledge about different names for drugs, or how they are taken. Further information on these is given on page 6.

You may want to know more about the effects of drug taking. If so, turn to page 7.

Maybe you were surprised at the views held by other people about certain drugs. The activities on pages 4 and 5 look at this in more detail.

≫ Taking drugs is nothing new. Throughout history, society has tried to prevent the misuse of drugs by legal controls. How well do you know the present laws about drugs? Which of these are illegal?

● To give alcohol to anyone under five.

● To drink wine with a meal in a pub, if you are under 16.

● To grow cannabis in your own home/garden.

● For a family Doctor to prescribe amphetamines to help patients to lose weight.

In fact, *all* of these activities are *illegal*.

What might be the reasons for these laws?

How easy is it to enforce these laws?

What are your own views about the laws relating to drug misuse?

How well do you know the legal facts about drugs? Agencies which could give you more information are listed on page 27.

Attitudes to Different Drugs

We often hold different views about particular drugs. To give an example, a person may think it is normal and acceptable to get drunk on a Saturday evening, but disapprove of anyone taking cannabis.

ACTIVITIES

» In order to be clearer about your attitudes and feelings to different drugs, join with two other people in a game of 'verbal tennis'.

The two players sit or stand facing each other. The third person is to be umpire. To get the idea of the game, the umpire should choose a topic or issue. Some ideas for topics are given in the left-hand box below.

The two players then take it in turns to say a word which fits that group.

They should keep going for as long as they can. Stop when one person runs out of ideas or repeats a word.

Next the umpire chooses one of the words in the *Legal* drug box.

Towns Football clubs Pop groups Insects Trees Birds Vegetables	**Legal** Alcohol Cigarettes Coffee Aspirin	**Illegal** Heroin Cannabis Ecstasy Amphetamines

Repeat the activity, with players calling out in turn any word which comes into their heads associated with that particular drug. The umpire should write down all the words which they call out.

Finally, select a word from the *Illegal* drug box and repeat the activity again.

Compare the lists of words which have been written about the two drugs. Are there any similarities or differences? If different views are held, where do these come from? Are they justified? If so, on what grounds? Do you need more information on the drugs concerned?

» On separate pieces of paper or card, write down the names of different drugs. (Look at page 6 if you are stuck for ideas.) You need enough pieces of card for the people in your group. Hand out one to each person.

Imagine that there is a line running up the centre of the room. At one end is 'Acceptable', at the other 'Unacceptable'.

Position yourself along this line according to the drug which you are holding. Discuss with those near you why you are standing there. You may find that you want to change places after discussion.

Once you are all satisfied with your positions, place the pieces of card on the floor in a line and stand back to see the final results. Are there any surprises? Have you learnt anything about the drugs your group chose; about yourself, about others in the group, as a result of doing this activity?

Popular images of drug users

ACTIVITY

This activity is intended to help you think about your image of users and non-users of various drugs. If possible pair up with someone else. Then complete the following sentences on your own as quickly as you can.

For example: People who smoke cigars are ... rich men.

People who take heroin are ...
People who sniff glue are ...
People who take tranquillizers are ...
People who drink are ...
People who don't drink are ...
People who smoke cannabis are ...
People who take ecstasy are ...
People who smoke cigarettes are ...
People who don't smoke are ...
People who don't take heroin are ...

Compare your results with your partner. What is the general picture that you have? Are some drugs associated with men and some with women? Are some associated with the wealthy and some with people on low incomes? Are some more likely to be taken by people in certain age groups?

How much do you know about drugs and the different people who use them? The next few pages explore this in more detail.

Different Drugs

Drug	Street name	How it is taken
Alcohol: Gin, Whisky, Beer, Vodka, Martini, Cider, Sherry, Wine	Drink, Booze	Swallowed as liquid
Amphetamines: Dexedrine, Benzedrine, Driamyl, Amphetamine Sulphate	'Uppers', 'Sweets', Speed, Whizz, Dexies, Bennies	Swallowed as pills. In powder form, snorted up the nose, stirred into a drink, or prepared for injection
Barbiturates: Seconal, Nembutal	Sleeping pills, Sleepers, Downers	Swallowed as pills
Caffeine: Coffee, Tea	Char	Swallowed as a drink
Cannabis, Marijuana, Cannabis resin, Cannabis oil	Smoke, Blow, Weed, Pot, Hash, Hay, Joint, Grass, Dope	Smoked in a joint. Sometimes eaten raw or as an ingredient in cooking
Cocaine, Crack	Coke, Charlie, Snow	Injected, sniffed, smoked
Ecstasy: MDMA	E, love doves, disco biscuits, big brownies, flat liners	Swallowed as tablets or capsules
Heroin, Opium, Morphine, Diconal, Distalgesic	Smack, Horse, 'H', Skag, Harry, Gear	Smoked, swallowed, sniffed, injected
Ketamine	K, Special K, Quick	Powder is usually sniffed up the nose, but can be prepared for injection. Tablets are swallowed
LSD: Lysergic Acid	Acid, Hawk, Cheer, Tabs, Microdot, Stars, Strawberries	Swallowed as pill, or sometimes as liquid on paper squares
Magic mushrooms, Liberty cap mushroom		Taken fresh, cooked or brewed in tea. Preserved by drying
Poppers: amyl or butyl nitrate	Liquid gold, TNT, rush	Vapours from the liquid are inhaled through the nose or into the mouth
Solvents: Glue, Lighter fuel, Aerosol, Dry cleaning fluid, Nail varnish remover		Sniffed
Tobacco: Cigarettes, Cigars, Pipe tobacco, Snuff	Fags	Smoked, sniffed, chewed
Tranquillizers: Valium, Librium, Altuan	Tranx, Downers	Taken as pills

What do you know?

How much do you know about the effects of drugs?

For each numbered statement below, put a ring round T if you think it is TRUE or round F if you think it is FALSE.

1	A drug is any substance that causes changes in the body or mind.	T	F
2	As a rule, women need less alcohol than men to get drunk.	T	F
3	Someone who drinks several cups of coffee a day will suffer no side-effects if they give it up.	T	F
4	Cigarette smokers only harm themselves.	T	F
5	A few drops of nicotine on the tongue will kill a healthy adult.	T	F
6	Taking cannabis affects the memory.	T	F
7	For some people taking drugs makes life more enjoyable.	T	F
8	There is no harm in mixing tranquillizers and alcohol.	T	F
9	The first time you inject heroin, you become addicted to it.	T	F
10	Only a few drugs are dangerous during pregnancy.	T	F
11	Cocaine is not a highly addictive drug.	T	F
12	People who only drink beer cannot become alcoholics.	T	F
13	Cannabis smoking can damage the lungs.	T	F
14	Once an addict always an addict.	T	F
15	LSD causes hallucinations.	T	F
16	Heroin is only addictive when it is injected – smoking it is fine.	T	F
17	You can do things better after a few drinks.	T	F
18	Tranquillizers reduce anxiety and tension.	T	F
19	Most glue-sniffing deaths result from the poisonous effects of the substance used.	T	F
20	You can become HIV positive by taking drugs.	T	F
21	Black coffee sobers you up if you have been drinking.	T	F
22	Taking steroids can cause a man's genitals to shrink and a woman's to enlarge.	T	F
23	The same drug can affect you differently, at different times.	T	F

How Did You Rate?

Check how right you were with the answers set out here.

1 **True**   A drug is any substance which alters the way in which the body works.

No matter how a drug is taken, it finds its way into the bloodstream and is carried in the blood to the brain. The brain is linked to all parts of the body via nerves which carry messages through electrical impulses. At the same time messages are carried back to another part of the brain where a sensation is produced.

Different drugs will affect different parts of the body. Certain drugs will cause harm to particular organs, for example the liver is damaged by alcohol, the lungs by nicotine, the stomach by aspirins, the heart by solvents.

2 **True**   For two reasons: a) women usually weigh less than men, b) men have a higher proportion of water in their bodies than women, so the alcohol is more diluted.

3 **False**   Coffee contains a drug called Caffeine. People who drink coffee regularly will become dependent upon it and when they give it up they may suffer from headaches, sweating, anxiety and vomiting.

4 **False**   Inhaling tobacco smoke from other people's cigarettes can harm the lungs. This is called 'passive smoking' and is the reason why smoking is banned in public places.

5 **True**   Pure nicotine is a highly poisonous substance. Very small amounts can cause severe illness.

6 **True**   Small to moderate doses of cannabis can affect a person's memory. It is more common among regular, heavy users of cannabis, where it also affects the ability to concentrate.

7 **True**   If you are ill, certain drugs can relieve pain, e.g. morphine is used to help people suffering from cancer. Many people enjoy taking drugs, such as alcohol at social occasions.

8 **False**   Taking any drugs together is highly dangerous. It is not a good idea to mix alcohol with any drug, because it will affect the way the drug works.

9 **False**   Not everyone becomes addicted to heroin. However, tolerance (i.e. reduced sensitivity to the drug) builds up very rapidly and larger doses have to be taken to produce the same effect, leading to addiction.

10 **False**   It is not advisable to take any drugs during pregnancy or if intending to get pregnant. Recent studies have shown that smoking can cause low birth weight in babies. It is also best to avoid alcohol during pregnancy.

11 **False**   Cocaine is more usually sniffed or 'snorted' and rapidly produces feelings of physical and mental power and indifference to pain and fatigue. Withdrawal causes depression, tiredness and

inability to cope with work. The user rapidly becomes 'dependent in their mind' on the drug, although there is no physical dependence.

12 **False** It is not what you drink, but how much you drink that is important. Half a pint of beer has the same alcohol content as a single whisky.

13 **True** There is a risk of lung or bronchial damage when smoking cannabis – in the same way that cigarette smoking harms the lungs.

14 **False** There are many cases of people who are successful in breaking their dependency on drugs. Many find it most difficult to stay off drugs as it means changing their way of life completely.

15 **True** The effect of LSD can vary according to the mind of the user. It has a powerful effect on the way people see and hear things. They will also have hallucinations, i.e. see and hear things that are not there. This can be very frightening. People may do extraordinary things when having a 'bad trip', often causing harm to themselves.

16 **False** Heroin is addictive, no matter how it is taken. Frequent use increases 'tolerance' to the drug leading to dependency and addiction.

17 **False** People drinking think they are able to do things better, e.g. a man may feel more inclined to have sex, but be less able to do so!

18 **True** Tranquillizers might make you feel good for a short while, but they do not do anything to solve the problem causing the anxiety and tension.

19 **False** Most deaths from glue-sniffing (solvent abuse) are the result of asphyxiation and suffocation, due to choking on vomit. There have also been what are called 'sudden sniffing deaths', from respiratory arrest.

20 **True** If you share needles to inject drugs with someone who already has the HIV virus, it means you are likely to become infected yourself and may develop AIDS later.

21 **False** It may stop you feeling drowsy, but it will not speed up the time taken for the liver to burn off the alcohol and will not lower your blood alcohol level.

22 **True** In men, steroids can decrease hormone levels and sperm production and at the same time cause breast development. In women, use of steroids can bring about hair growth or baldness and the deepening of the voice. Menstruation may become irregular or stop altogether and breasts may shrink. Long-term use can also result in liver tumours.

23 **True** How drugs affect us at any particular time depends upon:
how much has been taken
whether a person is a regular user
a person's mind – what the person expects to feel
the situation and company they are in.

Facts About Drug Use

It is very difficult to work out precisely the number of people using a particular drug. Often we rely on surveys which ask people questions such as 'which of the following drugs have you tried?' or 'how often do you take ...?' The accuracy of the results depends on people's honesty. Often if people feel guilty about taking drugs, they try to pretend it hasn't happened. For example, someone with a drink problem will deny that anything is wrong, although it might be affecting their family and work.

Some other ways of collecting information about drug use

Doctors have to notify the Home Office of anyone addicted to narcotic drugs (e.g. heroin).

The numbers of people found guilty of or cautioned for drug offences.

The quantity of illegal drugs seized by Customs and Excise.

The quantity of prescriptions handed in for drugs which act on the nervous system (e.g. tranquillizers).

The revenue in taxes from alcohol and cigarettes.

Causes of death on death certificates.

The 'facts' that we remember often come from articles or reports in newspapers, magazines, the radio or television. We need to be careful if we are to distinguish the 'facts' from sensational reporting.

A WHOLE NEIGHBOURHOOD COLLAPSED IN ADDICTION

COCAINE UNLIMITED

POLICE RAID ACID HOUSE PARTY

EVIL drugs parties are taking over in the South

Britain under threat from US drug craze

DRUG dealers are out to get children under ten

Of all 16-18 year old drivers killed almost half had been drinking too much

ALCOHOL CAN AFFECT UNBORN BABIES

If we put all the pieces of information together from various sources, we begin to get a more complete picture.

Take the year 1987, in the UK (Population = 56.9 million people: 20 per cent under 16; 64 per cent between 16 and 64; 16 per cent over 65.)

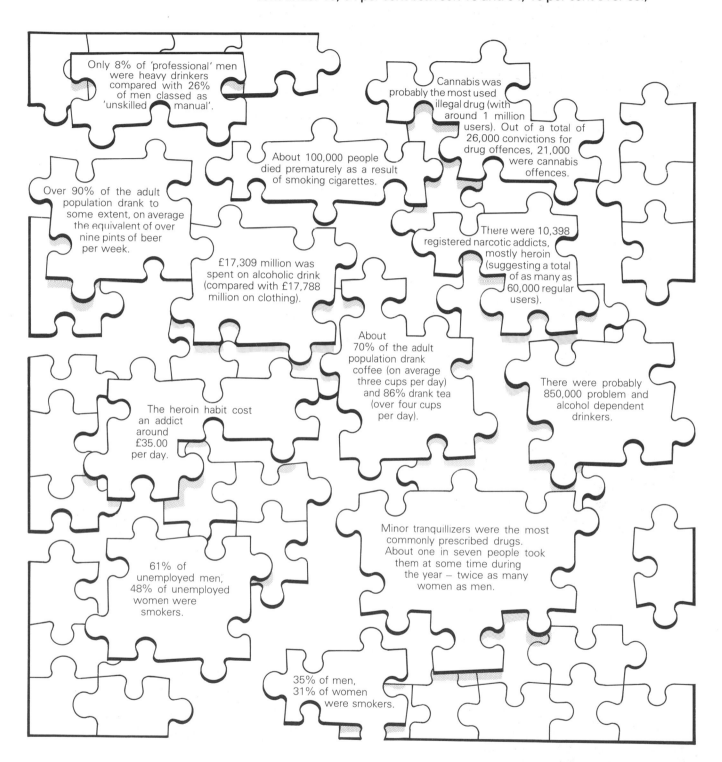

Only 8% of 'professional' men were heavy drinkers compared with 26% of men classed as 'unskilled manual'.

Cannabis was probably the most used illegal drug (with around 1 million users). Out of a total of 26,000 convictions for drug offences, 21,000 were cannabis offences.

About 100,000 people died prematurely as a result of smoking cigarettes.

Over 90% of the adult population drank to some extent, on average the equivalent of over nine pints of beer per week.

There were 10,398 registered narcotic addicts, mostly heroin (suggesting a total of as many as 60,000 regular users).

£17,309 million was spent on alcoholic drink (compared with £17,788 million on clothing).

About 70% of the adult population drank coffee (on average three cups per day) and 86% drank tea (over four cups per day).

There were probably 850,000 problem and alcohol dependent drinkers.

The heroin habit cost an addict around £35.00 per day.

Minor tranquillizers were the most commonly prescribed drugs. About one in seven people took them at some time during the year – twice as many women as men.

61% of unemployed men, 48% of unemployed women were smokers.

35% of men, 31% of women were smokers.

Can you answer the following questions:

1 In 1987, which seems to be the most used illegal drug?
2 Which was the most used legal drug?
3 Name one drug used more by women than men?
4 Name one drug used more by men than women?

Do any of these facts surprise you?

The Local Picture

How *much* a drug is used depends on a wide range of factors. The box below gives some of these.

Facts and figures about drug use nationally may not tell us very much about our local scene.

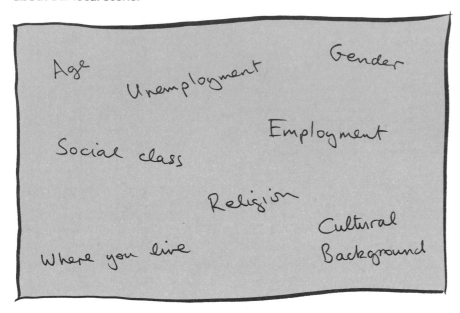

ACTIVITIES

» We may think we know how much a certain drug is used by people our own age. Choose a particular group of students (for example from one department, in your tutorial group, taking a certain subject, on day-release, the whole college).

Try to guess the percentage that smoke cigarettes:

● Every day
● Occasionally
● Never

Conduct a survey to test this out. How accurate was your guess? Did you tend to overestimate or underestimate? How honest do you think students were in their replies?

» Bring in a selection of local newspapers and cut out any articles about drugs. Working with two or three other people, can you group these articles according to the substances involved? Together answer the following questions.

Which substances are involved, e.g. heroin, valium or alcohol?
How often is the word drug mentioned?
Which adjectives are often used with it, e.g. 'dangerous', 'menace', 'killer'?
What effect is this type of media coverage likely to have on our views of different drugs?
What does it tell us about local drug use?

» Conduct a survey to assess local attitudes to drug-taking. The questionnaire on the next page offers some guidelines on possible questions. Perhaps you can think of others.

What do others think?

How do your ideas on drugs compare with other people's? What do you think springs to mind when people hear the word *drug*?

This questionnaire will help you to find out. Try using it with at least four people of different ages.

Questionnaire

1 Can you name *six* different drugs?

a _____   d _____

b _____   e _____

c _____   f _____

2 Which of the following words come to mind when you hear the word *drug*? Ring around your answers.

Harmful   Exciting   Habit   Risky

Painkilling   Fun   Relaxing

Expensive   Addicted

Injecting   Smoking

High

3 Can you add two other words of your own?

_____   _____

4 Which of the following legal drugs do you think are most used in your neighbourhood?

Tea   Alcohol   Cigarettes

Coffee   Sleeping pills   Aspirin

5 Have you ever been offered an illegal drug? YES/NO

6 If YES, do you know what it was?

7 Do you personally know anyone taking an illegal drug? YES/NO

8 If YES, do you know what it is?

If you compare the answers that different people have given, is there any difference in the replies given by people of different ages?

● What did people mention first – legal or illegal drugs?

● Which illegal drugs do people mention from their own experience?

What's The Harm?

'What's the harm?' 'Anyway, it'll never happen to me.' 'It's a lot of fuss about nothing.'

Is too much fuss made about drug taking? Let us look at *alcohol*, a drug we all know well. When people drink is it always just a case of having fun, relaxing and enjoying yourself? Look at the people in the situations below. What do you think the person looking on is thinking? Copy the bubbles and fill them with your suggestions for captions.

Choose one situation and think of the possible consequences for the people involved.

How many of the consequences you have identified are positive? How many negative?

What's your limit?

There are various laws aimed at reducing the harm caused by alcohol. For example, it is illegal to drive with a BAC greater than 80mg/100ml. But what does this mean?

BAC = Blood alcohol concentrate

When a drink containing alcohol is swallowed, it reaches the stomach and the alcohol passes into the small intestine and into the blood. The amount of alcohol in the blood is known as the BAC. It is measured in milligrammes of alcohol per 100 millilitres of blood and is usually written mg/100ml.

Your BAC will depend on a number of factors:

● *How much you weigh*: Large people contain more blood and body fluids than small people. Therefore, the same amount of alcohol will produce a lower BAC in large people than in small ones.

● *Your sex*: women are more easily affected than men because they have proportionally less body water.

● *The number and type of alcoholic drinks consumed*: some drinks have a higher concentration than others. One unit of alcohol is contained in the following measures of these drinks.

one glass of wine = half a pint of ordinary beer = one glass of sherry = one pub measure of spirits

● *The amount of food in the stomach*: if there is food in the stomach, the alcohol is absorbed into the blood more slowly.

● *The rate at which drinks are consumed*: as a rough guide, it takes around one hour for the alcohol to be absorbed and for the BAC to reach its peak. Once it has been absorbed, the liver gradually burns it up at a rate of 15mg per hour, i.e. the equivalent of half a pint of beer.

People who are regular drinkers become less affected by alcohol as their bodies become used to it. However their BAC will be the same as a person who only drinks occasionally. The danger is that the regular drinker needs to drink more to get the same effect.

Why Do It?

The people pictured below are all taking legal drugs for different reasons.

What are people's reasons for taking drugs? If possible, work with someone else to list as many reasons as you can think of.

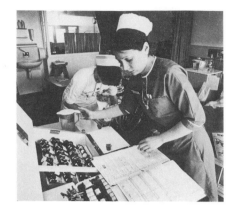

Compare your list with the list below.

Reasons people have given for taking drugs:

to feel more relaxed	it's the done thing	I like the taste
to give me a boost	to be a rebel	I was thirsty
to help me sleep	to give myself a treat	to relieve a hangover
someone offered	to relieve pain	to have a good laugh
I was bored	it goes down well with a meal	to give me confidence
to forget problems	to be different	to be one of the crowd
to perform sexually	to relieve stress	to see what it's like

Now take Karen, 19 years-old, who uses drugs for a variety of reasons:

recreational ('I like to go for a drink with my friends')
experimental ('I want to lose weight, so I'll try some of those pills')
regular ('When I start a period, I take a pain killer')
habitual ('I always start the day with a cup of coffee')
problem ('I wish I could give up cigarettes but I really need them')

If you use drugs it doesn't mean you have a 'problem'. Similarly no one becomes a problem drug-user overnight. How might it happen? If we think of Karen and cigarettes . . . one step led to another.

> 66 *Most people use more than one drug a week.* 99

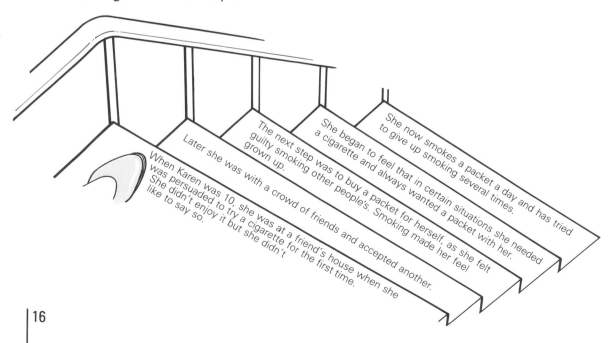

When Karen was 10, she was at a friend's house when she was persuaded to try a cigarette for the first time. She didn't enjoy it but she didn't like to say so.

Later she was with a crowd of friends and accepted another.

The next step was to buy a packet for herself, as she felt guilty smoking other people's. Smoking made her feel grown up.

She began to feel that in certain situations she needed a cigarette and always wanted a packet with her.

She now smokes a packet a day and has tried to give up smoking several times.

■ ACTIVITY

When are you most likely to take a drug, for example alcohol, cigarettes or cannabis? Here is a list of situations when people sometimes use drugs. How about you? Go down the list and tick the appropriate column for each situation.

	Would definitely not	Unlikely	Perhaps	Likely	Would definitely
1 When you are depressed. (Imagine a close relationship has just broken up.)					
2 When you want to be part of a group, to be friendly. (Imagine the first week in a new job – a crowd from work ask you to join them for a drink.)					
3 At the end of a tense day, when you are uptight.					
4 When faced with something that you are worried about. (Imagine the week or night before an exam or an interview that is important to you.)					
5 When you want to feel high and enjoy yourself.					
6 When you have to meet people that you do not know well. (Imagine going to a party or club where you will not know many people.)					
7 When you feel bad about yourself, feeling you are not as good as other people.					

Compare your results with someone else. Discuss these points:

● Did you have any particular drug in mind when you answered?
● Are your results similar?
● Could you imagine yourself ever taking an illegal drug?
● Can you imagine a situation when you might be offered an illegal drug?

Taking drugs does not automatically lead to problems. However, warning bells should perhaps ring if you feel that you have no other choice than to take a drug, e.g. if you need several pints before you can face people at parties. Choose one or two of the situations from the table above and think of other things that you could do to get the same effect, besides taking drugs. How realistic are these alternatives?

The Offer

Most of you have probably been offered some kind of drug at one time or another.

There may be many things which influence whether you accept or not.
You may need to ask some of the following questions.

Can you add any other questions?

Just say no – how easy is it?

In 1986, Esther Rantzen launched the *Drugwatch* project on BBC television. Various celebrities showed their support by signing their names under 'Just Say No'.

But how easy is it to say no when you find yourself in a situation where drugs are available?

Take the following situation:

> Alan has spent the evening with two friends in a pub. At closing time they go on to a party, where he knows a lot of the people. His friends start chatting to two girls and Alan drifts off to talk with another group. After a while, one of them asks, 'Has anyone got any grass?' A joint is handed round. Alan doesn't want to accept. What will he do?

ACTIVITIES

» Working with 2 or 3 others, list all the possible things which Alan could say or do. The following might be a start:

● Takes it as he doesn't want to be the odd one out.

● Tells the person offering it to 'get lost'.

● Says 'thanks for the offer, but NO'.

● ....

● ....

In every situation, it could be said that there are three possible ways of responding. You could be Assertive, Aggressive or Passive.

Assertive	= saying what you want to happen, while showing consideration for others.
Aggressive	= trying to get what you want, without consideration for others.
Passive	= doing nothing or hoping someone else will do it for you, not standing up for yourself.

Which of the responses you have listed is assertive? Which is aggressive? Which is passive?

Remember, *how* you say something often affects whether *what* you say is aggressive, assertive or passive. Even the simple words 'no thanks' can be spoken in various ways!

Which of these do you think would be the best way for Alan to handle the situation? Would this depend on anything, for example who he was with?

» In pairs, list all the arguments used to persuade people to take both legal and illegal drugs. Choose an argument that would be difficult to resist. Write it on a piece of paper and pass it to another pair. This pair should try to identify ways of dealing with it.

As a group, share your ideas for handling the different arguments.

Feeling **G**ood **A**bout **Y**ourself

If you want to be assertive in a certain situation, you need to feel that you have a right to get what you want. You need confidence in yourself and in your value, or you will tend not to stand up for yourself.

▓ ACTIVITIES

>> It is sometimes difficult to recognize your own good points. Try the exercise below. Write down five things which you like about yourself.

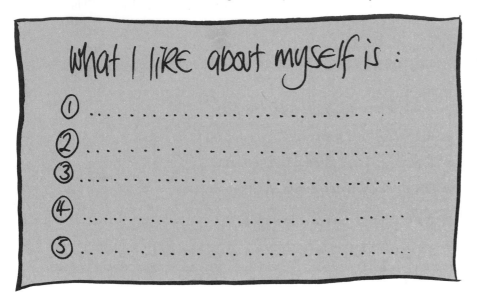

How easy did you find this to do? In our society, people are brought up not to boast or to be big-headed. We tend to feel uneasy about saying what we think we are good at. We may undervalue some qualities at the expense of others, e.g. overrating the ability to pass exams and get qualifications as opposed to the ability to help others feel at ease.

What are the skills or qualities in our society which tend to be discounted or ignored? Why might this be so?

>> Can you think of any situations where you have felt better about yourself because of the way in which someone has treated you? For example, when someone has shown that they valued your opinion. In pairs, list as many ways as possible of helping others to feel good about themselves.

Being assertive

An assertive response is not always appropriate. Sometimes it may be better to be passive or even aggressive. However, it is important to be able to *choose* how you respond, rather than always behaving in the same way. Perhaps we all know people who constantly fly off the handle, or who bully and tease. Similarly, others who never seem to stand up for themselves and who let people walk all over them. If you *do* want to be more assertive, what do you need to do?

Before you start

● You need to be sure of what you want to say or do.

● You need to feel that you have a right to say or do what you want – that your feelings and wishes are worth consideration.

What you say

● State your position clearly and concisely.

● Give your reason – but don't get drawn into lengthy explanation and arguments.

● Show that you appreciate the other person's feelings, e.g. 'It was good of you to offer'.

How you say it

● Say it as if you mean it – don't mumble or hesitate.

● Make sure the expression on your face matches what you are saying.

● Don't avoid looking at the person involved – on the other hand, don't stare fixedly at them!

● Make sure your body looks relaxed – don't shift from one foot to another, or fidget or chew your nails. If you do, you'll seem unsure of yourself.

ACTIVITY

The best way to practise being assertive is to try it out and to get someone else's opinion of how well it went and of how you came across.

〉 Work in groups of three with two of you pretending to be in a certain situation, and one observing. The observer should concentrate on the player trying to be assertive and should be prepared to say at the end of the conversation, how s/he appeared, e.g. how s/he was sitting or standing, leaning forward or back, arms crossed or uncrossed, looking at the other person or at the floor.
Try one of the following situations – or choose one of your own in which you would find it difficult to be assertive.

A doesn't like people smoking in her/his car. *B* goes to light up a cigarette.

A wants *B* to have an alcoholic drink, as s/he doesn't like drinking alone. *B* doesn't want one.

A is worried because s/he has a job interview tomorrow. *B* offers *A* some pills to help her/him to sleep. *A* doesn't want to accept.

〉 After two or three minutes, the observer should stop the conversation. Discuss in your threes:

● How each player felt.
● What they found difficult or easy.
● What made them feel good or angry.
● What the observer noticed.
● Whether a compromise was reached. Being assertive does not always mean winning.

Who **G**ains

Illegal drugs

> A man was sentenced at the Old Bailey yesterday for his part in a Mafia plot to supply £10 million of cocaine to dealers in this country.

Here are some responses to instances of large-scale illegal trading in drugs, like the example above.

'They should stop it coming in.'

'Heavier fines and jail sentences would soon put an end to it.'

'I blame the parents myself – if it weren't for them, there wouldn't be any customers for the stuff.'

'The police cannot tackle the problem on their own – they need greater support.'

'Anyone can get hold of drugs nowadays – huge profits are made all the time.'

'No wonder the crime figures are going up all the time.'

Medicines Act, 1986. This governs the manufacture and supply of medicinal products of all kinds, e.g. valium or antibiotics.

Misuse of Drugs Act, 1971. Amended in 1986 – this aims to prevent unauthorized use and misuse of drugs.

1 **Class A**: highest penalties – Heroin, Cocaine, LSD.
2 **Class B**: lower penalties – Amphetamines, Cannabis.
3 **Class C**: lowest penalties – Distalgesics, Librium, Valium.

Who gains – count the cost!

It might begin with a Pakistani hill farmer producing a crop of opium poppies, which helps him support a large family. This crop produces the highest return for his family and the other villagers. He may be unaware what happens to the crops later.

A drug producer in a local town in Pakistan, makes a good living from processing the opium poppy crop in to pure heroin. His outlay of £200.00 per kilo gives him a return of £5000 per kilo – a good profit! If he mixed the heroin with other substances, he could make even more. It's a risky life and he could end up in prison.

His customers are an international drug smuggling ring. He knows little about their organization.

As one of a drug smuggling ring, this woman lives dangerously. She has been paid up to £5000 per shipment of heroin that she has smuggled through customs. She finds it difficult to give up the life now she is so heavily involved. She is only a go-between obeying instructions.

As head of the organization, the profits received are huge and far outweigh the risks taken. The heroin entering the country is broken down, mixed with other substances and distributed widely. Each kilo of heroin can raise up to £80000 on the open market – there seems no end to the demand. The huge profits may be used to run legitimate businesses. Only 10 per cent brought into the country is seized by customs/police.

The pusher runs a network of street suppliers. Many of them have been drawn in to the net in order to maintain their own drug habit, and have begun a life of crime as a result.

The first shot of heroin was at a party, offered by a friend. The effect was good, it made him feel terrific and all his worries vanished. Now he needs it regularly. He is in serious trouble. The habit is costing him more and more each week from a street supplier. Stealing is the only way he can maintain his habit now he is hooked.

- In 1991, 2434 people were in prison for drug offences. Of these, 106 were aged under 21.
- Over recent years the number of drug offences identified by police and customs officers has continued to increase, doubling between 1986 and 1991.
- Unlawful production offences, including offences of cultivation of cannabis plants, fell between 1986 and 1991.
- Unlawful import of or export offences increased from 1525 in 1986 to 2136 in 1991.

In small groups discuss who you think is responsible for the great increase in the drug trade? Who are the winners? Who are the losers?

Make a list of your ideas about:
- How the supply of drugs might be controlled;
- How the demand might be controlled.

Legal Drugs

Perhaps you think that issues connected with illegal drugs have little to do with you. Maybe you are convinced that you will never take heroin, and think it unlikely that it will affect your life in any way.

But what about other drugs which are commonly used in our society? Have you ever thought of who gains from the sale of alcohol or cigarettes?

Some of the people who benefit from the sale of 'beer' are shown below.

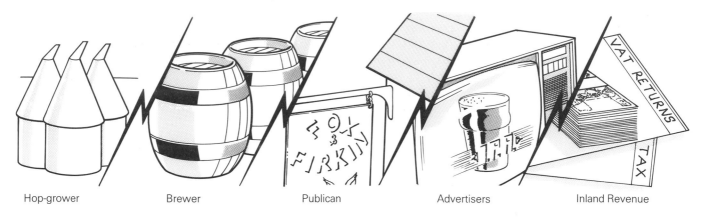

| Hop-grower | Brewer | Publican | Advertisers | Inland Revenue |

ACTIVITIES

» Find out figures for the profits made from the sale of cigarettes. You could contact ASH for information, see page 27.

» Cigarette advertising is banned on TV, but cigarette manufacturers find ways of getting round this through sport sponsorship. A report in 1986 stated that

'TV is now providing an average of almost one hour of tobacco sponsored programmes per evening (over 300 hours in a year) and within this overall programme time, about 2 to 6 minutes exposure per hour of the tobacco brand names; in darts the players smoke on TV continually; in snooker they smoke in front of the tobacco company's sign boards.'

(Source: *Code Busting by tobacco companies*, by J.L. Roberts, a report for the HEC, from the N.W. Regional Health Authority)

Carry out your own survey on sports events on BBC television, sponsored by tobacco companies. Look out for some of the following:

● Is the tobacco company's name mentioned in adverts for the programme?

● Is the name near the score-board?

● How many camera shots do you see of the tobacco company name?

● What length of time is each camera shot showing the name?

● Are the players seen smoking and for how long?

● Is there a health warning shown on tobacco boards?

● The colours or logos of the tobacco brands concerned: Are they used to decorate the setting? Do the players/referee/umpire wear the company's logo/colours?

Other influences

The following quotes are taken from *What is to be done about Illness and Health? Crisis in the Eighties,* by Jeannette Mitchell.

'I suffer with my chest and have a bit of difficulty getting about. I must be honest about this. It must be in part due to the fact that I smoke ... I think that far less people would smoke if they were not under stress and strain, as the average tenant is today through unemployment, marital problems and so on. Picking up a cigarette and having a draw, knowing it perhaps could do you harm, does not deter you. It becomes as Valium to a person who is undergoing sleepless nights.'

'I think the work was stressful. You just have to close your brain and try and make it happy. And think of Friday when you get your wage. Without that you can't live. When they are at home people are bored and then when they come into the factory they are bored. Then they become more depressed. There is no escape.'

How healthy or unhealthy we are is closely tied up with our work and home lives. Our use of drugs is also likely to be affected by whether we are employed or unemployed, by the type of work we do and by the conditions in which we live.

Looking at the table below you will see that cigarette smoking has decreased steadily from 1972 to 1990.

Smoking by sex and socio-economic group in Great Britain 1972–1984

Year	Socio-economic group					
	Professional	Employers and managers	Skilled manual	Semi-skilled manual	Unskilled manual	All aged 16 and over
Men	%	%	%	%	%	%
1972	33	44	57	57	64	52
1976	25	38	51	53	58	46
1978	25	37	49	53	60	45
1980	21	35	48	49	57	42
1984	17	29	40	45	49	36
1988	16	26	39	40	43	33
1990	16	24	36	39	48	31
Women	%	%	%	%	%	%
1972	33	38	47	42	42	42
1976	28	35	42	41	38	38
1978	23	33	42	41	41	37
1980	21	33	43	39	41	37
1984	15	29	37	37	36	32
1988	17	26	35	37	39	30
1990	16	23	32	36	36	29

(Source: General Household Survey for 1990)

However, the table shows that there is always a contrast in the numbers of people smoking in the unskilled manual group compared with the professional group. For example in 1990, 48 per cent of unskilled manual men smoked compared with only 16 per cent of professional men.

ACTIVITY

Working in small groups, think of some reasons for the difference in numbers shown above? The following questions may help in your discussions:

Are some people's lives more stressful?
Are some people influenced by the behaviour of those around them?
Are some people less aware of the dangers of smoking?

What If?

People sometimes find themselves in situations where drugs are causing problems, either for themselves or for others. It may be difficult to resolve these problems on their own. They may need more information, to talk it over with others, or to get outside help.

ACTIVITY

> Working with two or three others, choose one of the following dilemmas. Try to decide on the various courses of action open to the person concerned. There may not be one easy solution.

> The information given opposite provides some useful addresses of organizations to go to for help.

> For each course of action, check out:

Whether you have the necessary information. If not, where can you get it?
Whether, if you were in that situation, you would want to get involved or would you be more likely to ignore it and feel that it was none of your business?
Whether it is a situation that you can handle on your own, or whether you need other people's help.
The likely consequences or outcomes.

Dilemma 1
Your friend has exams coming up and is getting very depressed and worried. She has managed to get some tranquillizers. You are concerned that she is taking too many and that she might even attempt suicide. What are you going to do?

Dilemma 2
You are at a party with a group of friends. Most people have been drinking heavily and you've heard that a group upstairs have been taking illegal drugs. Towards the end a girl near you is found to be unconscious. What could be the reasons for this? What would be the best thing to do?

Dilemma 3
Your father lost his job last year. He has been getting more and more depressed and has become a heavy drinker. He says the pub is all he has to look forward to. Your mother is worried and angry about the amount he is spending. She has threatened to leave. Who could you turn to for help? Is there anything you can do to ease the situation?

Dilemma 4
You're at a rave. A friend of yours has taken two ecstasy tablets and decides he needs more. It's very hot and he's not been drinking much. What are you going to do?

Working as a small group, think of another possible 'dilemma', which might face people of your age. Write this on a slip of paper.

Collect all the slips together and choose someone to read them out. Are there any similarities in your ideas?

Choose the one which is of most interest to everyone, and share ideas on the possible solutions to it.

Any Help?

Most of the agencies listed on this page could put you in touch with groups/help in your area.

---

1 *Agencies if you yourself have a drug problem*

Accept Services, 724 Fulham Road, London SW6 5SE (Tel: 071 371 7477). Offers counselling and treatment for problem drinkers, tranquillizer misusers and their families. There are groups and clubs around the country. A wide variety of publications are available.

Alcoholics Anonymous (AA), PO Box 1, Stonebow House, Stonebow, York YO2 INJ (Tel: 0904 644026). For people who need help because of a problem with their drinking. Local branches are in the telephone book. AA hold regular confidential group meetings.

Narcotics Anonymous, PO Box 417, London SW10 (Tel: 071 351 6794/6066). Self-help groups are run by recovered addicts to help others recover from drug addiction. Meetings and contacts can be found in different parts of the country.

MIND (National Association for Mental Health), 22 Harley Street, London W1N 2ED (Tel: 071 6376 0741). This is a national organization co-ordinating tranquillizer withdrawal self-help groups throughout the country.

---

2 *Information on drugs and services*

Action on Smoking and Health (ASH), 109 Gloucester Place, London W1H 3PH (Tel: 071 935 3519). Provides information on the effects of smoking and health, and on how to give up. They also produce a free information pack.

Standing Conference on Drug Abuse (SCODA), 1–4 Hatton Place, Hatton Garden, London EC1N 8ND (Tel: 071 430 2341). SCODA is the national co-ordination body for voluntary organizations and agencies working in the drugs field. Regional field-workers keep in touch with developments and a news-letter is published on a regular basis.

Institute for the Study of Drug Dependence, 1–4 Hatton Place, Hatton Garden, London EC1N 8ND (Tel: 071 430 1993). Publishes up-to-date material on various aspects of the use and misuse of drugs.

Teachers' Advisory Council on Alcohol and Drug Education, (TACADE) 1 Hulme Place, The Crescent, Salford M5 4QA (Tel: 061 745 8925). Provides a wide range of publications on the use and misuse of drugs.

---

3 *Agencies if you have a friend or relative with a drug problem*

Al-Anon Family Groups UK & EIRE, 61 Great Dover Street, London SE1 4YF (Tel: 071 403 0388). A national network of self-help groups for relatives, friends and colleagues of problem drinkers.
Alateen is a part of Al-Anon, specifically to help young people who have an alcoholic parent or other relative or friend.

---

4 *Counselling (not just about drugs)*

National Association of Young People's Counselling and Advisory Service, Magazine Business Centre, 11 Newark St., Leicester LE1 5SS. Provides information on counselling and advisory service for young people throughout the country. Letter service only.

Samaritans, 10 The Grove, Slough SL1 1QP (Tel: 0753 32713). Offers a 24-hour free, confidential service to help the suicidal and despairing. See telephone directory for local numbers.

---

5 *Emergency Advice*

If you find a friend unconscious after taking drugs.

Call an ambulance or doctor – don't waste any time. Turn them on their side – don't let them lie on their backs. Loosen any clothing which is tight.

Don't give them anything to eat and don't give them tea, coffee or alcohol.

If they are overheated, move them into a cool place, splash them with cold water and fan them to cool them down.

Harm Reduction

People hold different views about how the harm caused by drugs could be reduced.

Which of the following do you agree with? Tick the appropriate box for each of the lettered statements.

	Strongly Agree	1	2	3	4	Strongly Disagree
a Smoking should be banned in public places.						
b The price of cigarettes should be increased.						
c The relaxation of licensing laws encourages a responsible attitude to alcohol.						
d There should not be sponsorship of sporting events by cigarette manufacturers.						
e There should be heavier penalties for shopkeepers who sell glue to children.						
f The tax on spirits should be increased.						
g Cannabis should be legalized.						
h The police should have the power to carry out random breathalyser tests.						
i Doctors should be discouraged from prescribing tranquillizers.						
j Free needles should be given to drug addicts to avoid the spread of AIDS.						
k All schools should provide education about drugs.						
l The Government should aim to improve housing conditions and to increase employment.						

Compare your results with a partner. Are there any statements where you have chosen very differently to them? Explain the reasons for your choices to one another.

It's Your Decision

1 Are you likely to take drugs?

3 If no, what do you need to do to be able to cope without drugs?

2 What information do you need before you make up your mind?

4 If yes, what do you need to do or know to be able to limit the damage of drug-taking?

If you *do* decide that you are going to use drugs, there are guidelines which you should bear in mind in order to reduce some of the risks.

Warnings

DON'T MIX DRUGS (for example pills and alcohol)

Alcohol
- The safe limit for alcohol is thought to be:
  for women – up to 14 units of alcohol a week;
  for men – up to 21 units of alcohol a week.
- Enjoy drink-free days.
- Don't drink and drive or operate machinery.
- Don't drink if you are pregnant.

Ecstasy/Amphetamines
- Drink at least a pint of water or lots of soft drinks every hour to avoid dehydration (not alcohol – it dehydrates even more).
- Don't dance for long periods. Take a break .
- Wear cool clothing. Don't wear a hat.
- Sit in a cool palace.

Prescribed pills
- Don't take pills prescribed for others.
- Even at low doses, your ability to drive or operate complicated machinery may be affected.

Cigarettes
- Smoke less – save your money and your health.
- Don't smoke if you are pregnant.

Heroin
- Don't share needles.
- Do you know what you are being offered?